A LITTL

COOKBOOK

MARILYN BRIGHT

Illustrated by JON BERKELEY

CHRONICLE BOOKS
SAN FRANCISCO

First published in 1994 by
The Appletree Press Ltd
19–21 Alfred Street
Belfast BT2 8DL
Tel. +44 232 243074 Fax +44 232 246756
Copyright © 1994 The Appletree Press, Ltd.
Illustrations © 1994 The Appletree Press, Ltd.
Printed in the E.C. All rights reserved.
No part of this publication may be reproduced or
transmitted in any form or by any means, electronic or
mechanical, photocopying, recording or any information
and retrieval system, without permission in writing from
the publisher.

A Little Provençal Cookbook

First published in the United States in 1994 by
Chronicle Books, 275 Fifth Street, San Francisco,
California 94103

ISBN 0-8118-0774-6

9 8 7 6 5 4 3 2 1

Introduction

It is hard not to fall in love with Provence at first sight. Sun, glittering sea, and herb-scented breezes combine with lush hillside groves, bustling seaports, and colorful markets to capture all the senses.

The food of Provence is rich in tradition, with many dishes inherited from ancient Rome and Phoenician antecedents, making use of sun-drenched local ingredients. The classic bags of *herbes de Provence* are mixtures of the native thyme, rosemary, bay, fennel, and oregano that grow on the hills. Along with garlic, olive oil, and olives, tomatoes, and anchovies, they appear repeatedly in Provençal recipes, providing an aromatic theme that is unmistakable.

Along the rocky shores of Provence, fish dishes such as the renowned *bouillabaisse* were born of the necessity to make up in flavor what the meager fish lacked in size. In this book we have done our best to interpret these unique dishes with ingredients that are available everywhere. Few Provençal cooks use written recipes, so our versions of dishes are meant to act as a guide in most cases. We encourage you to indulge your own creativity as a French cook would, adjusting amounts and flinging in olives or extra cloves of garlic to suit the day's larder or mood.

A note on measures
Spoon and dry cup measurements are level. Seasonings can be adjusted according to taste. Recipes are for four unless otherwise indicated.

Pistou

Taking its name from the Niçoise verb meaning "to pound", this wonderfully aromatic sauce is best handmade with a mortar and pestle. A popular summer seasoning for stirring into soup or hot cooked vegetables, it can be kept refrigerated in a jar for a few days if the top surface is sealed with a thin layer of olive oil.

---

2 cloves garlic
pinch of salt
large handful of fresh basil leaves
5 tbsp freshly grated Parmesan cheese
5 tbsp olive oil

With a mortar and pestle or in a bowl with a wooden spoon, crush the garlic to a paste with the salt, then add basil leaves and pound again. Stir in the Parmesan cheese and add olive oil slowly while stirring to make a smooth sauce.

Soupe au Pistou

Residents of Nice have their own version of minestrone based on small white haricot beans. This is a main course soup to be served with crusty French bread and freshly made *pistou* (see p. 4).

---

scant 1½ cups dried haricot beans, soaked overnight
2 cloves garlic, crushed
1 stalk celery, finely sliced
3 carrots, diced
2 leeks, sliced
1½ cups green beans
2 white turnips, diced
2 medium potatoes, diced
2 tomatoes, peeled and diced
1 cup peeled and diced pumpkin or squash
2 small zucchini, sliced
3 tbsp olive oil
salt and pepper
pistou (see p. 4)
freshly grated Parmesan cheese
(serves 6)

Put the soaked beans, garlic, and celery in fresh water and bring to a boil. Simmer until tender, about 1 hour. Add vegetables and olive oil and simmer over low heat until all are cooked, adding more water if needed. Season with salt and pepper to taste. Stir *pistou* into soup just before serving. If desired, serve with freshly grated Parmesan cheese on top.

Aioli

Aioli is a golden garlicky mayonnaise considered the queen of Mediterranean sauces. Sometimes called "the butter of Provence", it is traditionally served with boiled salt cod, hard-boiled eggs, and a selection of raw and cooked vegetables. The amount of garlic can be varied according to taste but Provençal cooks generally allow two cloves per person. It is important that all ingredients for the sauce are at warmish room temperature.

8–16 cloves of garlic, peeled
1/2 tsp salt
3 egg yolks
2 1/2 cups olive oil
3-5 tbsp lemon juice

Pound the garlic and the salt to a paste, then beat in the egg yolks. Beat in one-third of the olive oil drop by drop until the mixture thickens. Stir in the remaining oil in a thin stream. Add lemon juice to taste and adjust seasoning with more salt if needed.

Rouille

A peppery red sauce pungent with garlic, rouille is traditionally served with *bouillabaisse* (see p. 15) or one of the many varieties of fish soup cooked along the coast of southern France. It should be spread on a toasted round of bread and placed in the dish before the soup is ladled over.

---

1 small sweet red pepper, de-seeded and diced
1 red chilli pepper, de-seeded and chopped
2 cloves garlic, peeled
1 thick slice white bread, crustless
$^3/_4$ cup olive oil
salt
soup broth (optional)

Place the peppers and garlic in a food processor and blend to a paste. Soak the bread in water, squeeze the water out, and blend with the pepper mixture. Stir in the olive oil slowly until blended. Season to taste with salt. If desired, the sauce may be thinned with a little of the broth from the soup it is to be served with.

Aïgo Boulido

First-timers enjoying this flavorful soup will be amazed to find that it is garlic based. While cooking, this most pungent of herbs is mellowed to an indefinable aromatic deliciousness.

---

1 whole head of garlic
4 tbsp olive oil
bouquet garni: bay leaf, parsley, thyme, sage sprigs
2 cloves
7½ cups water
salt, pepper
3 egg yolks
French bread, sliced and toasted
grated cheese (optional)

Separate and peel garlic cloves and bruise slightly with side of knife. Heat olive oil in large pot and soften garlic for a minute or two without coloring. Add *bouquet garni*, cloves, water, and salt and pepper. Bring to a boil, then reduce heat and simmer for 30 minutes. Discard *bouquet garni* and cloves and purée the soup in a blender or food processor.

Beat egg yolks in the bottom of the warmed soup tureen. Reheat soup and beat a little of it drop by drop into the egg yolks. When a ladleful or so has been blended with the egg yolks, the remaining soup can be added. If reheating is necessary, do not allow it to boil. Adjust seasoning if necessary, place the toast in soup bowls and pour the soup over. If desired, serve with grated cheese.

Bouillabaisse

Purists say that this Provençal signature dish can only be made with freshly landed rock fish from the Mediterranean coast. Any good variety of fish and shellfish can produce pleasing results though, particularly if a good mix of soft fish (for melting into the soup) and firm fish (for chunky texture) is used Recommended varieties include cod, gurnet, sea bass, bream, monkfish, sole, perch, pollack, wrasse, hake, and halibut, and shellfish such as crab, lobster, scallops, and mussels.

---

5 lb small whole fish and chunks of large fish	2 tbsp olive oil
	2 small leeks, sliced
1 onion, roughly chopped	2 onions, finely chopped
bouquet garni: parsley, thyme, bay leaf	4 cloves garlic, crushed
9 cups water	1 lb tomatoes, chopped
1 tsp whole peppercorns	pinch of saffron
1 tsp salt	2 inch piece of orange peel
1 tsp fennel seeds, slightly crushed	

Clean and fillet the fish. Put fillets to one side and crush bones, heads, and trimmings into a large pot with the onion, *bouquet garni*, water, peppercorns, salt, and fennel seeds. Bring to a boil and simmer for 25 minutes. Strain off the stock and discard debris. Heat olive oil in a large pot and soften the leeks, onions, garlic, and tomatoes. Remove from heat and layer the fish fillets in pot, with the thicker, solid pieces on the bottom. Pour in the prepared stock, add saffron and orange peel. Simmer until all the fish is cooked through, 20-30 minutes. Taste and adjust seasoning. Serve over thick rounds of bread, with *rouille* (p. 11) passed separately or spread on toast.

Grilled Red Mullet with Fennel

Red mullet is considered one of the finest fish of the Mediterranean. It is gutted with its liver intact, as this is prized as a great delicacy. In the south, bunches of fennel branches are sold to serve as beds for grilling, but elsewhere bulb fennel makes a tasty alternative.

---

4 small red mullet
1 large or 2 small bulbs Florence fennel
4 tbsp olive oil
juice of 1 lemon
1 clove garlic, crushed
salt and pepper

Scale and clean mullet, leaving liver inside. Make several deep slashes through thickest part of fish. Trim fennel and cut lengthwise into flat slices. Beat remaining ingredients together to make basting sauce and brush over both sides of fennel slices and inside and outside fish. Broil fennel quickly on both sides, then lay fish on top and broil until done, about 25 minutes, turning once and basting from time to time.

Salade Niçoise

Black olives, tuna, and an aromatic vinaigrette dressing combine with summery vegetables for this main course that has travelled far from its sunny origins in Nice.

---

1 1/2 lb new potatoes
1 cup sauce vinaigrette (see p.20)
8 oz green beans
1 head loose-leaf lettuce, separated, washed and dried
4 tomatoes, quartered
7 1/2 oz can of tuna, drained
3 hard-boiled eggs, shelled and quartered
8 anchovy fillets, drained and chopped

Boil the unpeeled potatoes, taking care not to overcook. Drain, cut in half and dress with a little vinaigrette (p. 20) while still warm. Top and tail the beans and simmer in a saucepan in a little boiling water until just tender; drain and dress while still warm. Line a salad bowl with the lettuce leaves and arrange the salad ingredients attractively, ending with anchovy fillets scattered over top. Pour over remaining vinaigrette dressing.

Sauce Vinaigrette

Nearly every sort of raw and cooked vegetable is used for fresh tasting salads in Provence, enhanced by freshly made vinaigrette and aromatic herbs. Only wine vinegar and the best golden olive oil are used. The dressing may be whisked in a bowl, but is mixed easiest when shaken in a screw-top jar.

1/4 cup wine vinegar
3/4 cup good olive oil
1 tsp Dijon mustard
1/2 tsp salt
freshly ground black pepper
1 clove garlic, finely chopped
3 tbsp finely chopped fresh herbs of choice: basil, chervil chives,
parsley, tarragon, thyme
(makes about 1 cup)

Combine all ingredients in a screw-top jar and shake until thoroughly blended. Use as marinade for warm-cooked vegetables or pour over fresh salads just before serving.

Quichets aux Anchois

Anchoiade, a garlicky anchovy paste, is spread on crusty bread and grilled to make hot snacks that are delicious with drinks. The same mixture can be used as topping for potatoes or hard-boiled eggs.

---

1 can (2 oz) anchovies, drained
2 cloves garlic, chopped
4 tbsp olive oil
1 tbsp red wine vinegar
1 small baguette

Process all ingredients to a paste in a blender or by hand with a mortar and pestle. Split the baguette lengthwise and spread the *anchoiade* on each half, pressing well into the bread. Broil until mixture starts to bubble and color. Cut bread into pieces and serve hot.

Tapenade

Tapeno, the Provençal name for caper, lends its name to this wonderful savory paste of black olives, anchovies, and capers. It is most often used as a spread on toast or crusty French bread or as a topping for hard-boiled eggs. It keeps well in a jar in the refrigerator.

---

4 oz black olives, stoned
3 tbsp capers
I can (2 oz) anchovies, drained
$^1/_2$ clove garlic, chopped
I tbsp lemon juice
I tbsp brandy
$^1/_2$ cup olive oil

Combine all ingredients except olive oil in a blender and process while slowly pouring in olive oil. Finished mixture should be a slightly grainy paste.

Esquinado à l'Huile

Spider crab, called *esquinado* in Provence, is beaten with olive oil to make a tasty spread for toasted croutons or a sauce for plainly cooked white fish. Other types of crab can be used, preferably with a mixture of white and brown meat.

---

2 hard-boiled eggs
12 oz crab meat
juice of 1 lemon
1 tsp Dijon mustard
scant ⅔ cup olive oil
salt, pepper
finely chopped parsley

Peel and halve the eggs, remove yolks, finely chop the whites and reserve. Place cooked yolks in a food processor with the crab meat, lemon juice, mustard, and olive oil and blend to make a smooth paste. Season with salt and pepper. Serve in a shallow dish or in clean dry crab shells, decorating with the chopped egg whites and parsley.

La Bourride

Restaurants serve this fish dish and its garlicky sauce in individual casserole dishes, lifting the lid to release the delicious aroma at the table. Firm white fish such as halibut, monkfish, bass, hake, and turbot are suitable, and the dish should include a mixture of three types.

---

1 large onion, sliced
2 cloves garlic, crushed
1 tsp fennel seeds
1 1/4 cups white wine
2 1/2 cups fish stock
3 inch strip orange peel
2 lb firm white fish fillets
8 rounds toasted French bread
1 egg yolk
1 1/4 cups aioli (p. 8)
salt, pepper

Place the onion, garlic, and fennel seeds in a large skillet with the wine, fish stock, and orange peel. Bring to a boil, lay fish fillets in the skillet and simmer gently until just cooked. Carefully remove fish to a large serving dish, surround with toast and keep warm. Strain the cooking liquid and quickly reduce to about 1 1/2 cups. Beat the egg yolk into the *aioli* and then slowly whisk in the hot stock. Taste and season with salt and pepper. Pour over fish and toasted bread in serving dish.

Gigot à la Crème d'Ail

Provençal lambs graze on hillside meadows rich in wild herbs. In this recipe the lamb is further enhanced by prodigious amounts of garlic which mellow in the delicious cooking juices.

---

1 leg of lamb, boned
salt, pepper
1 tbsp chopped fresh thyme and rosemary
olive oil
1 lb garlic cloves, peeled
4-5 tbsp cream
rounds of toasted bread
(serves 6-8)

Preheat oven to 375°F. Open out the boned lamb, season with salt and pepper and scatter with chopped herbs. Roll and tie the joint. Heat olive oil in a flameproof casserole dish and brown joint on all sides. During final stages, add garlic cloves and allow to brown slightly. Cover the casserole dish, place in oven and cook lamb for 18-25 minutes per pound, depending on pinkness desired. When lamb is cooked, remove to serving dish and keep warm. Place garlic in food processor and purée with enough cream to make good spreading consistency. Carve the lamb in slices, pour the pan juices over it, and surround with the toasted bread spread with garlic cream.

Boeuf en Daube

A scattering of black olives gives this rich beef stew its special Provençal flavor. Around Nice it is usually served with fresh ribbon noodles.

---

3 tbsp olive oil
1 large onion, sliced
3 cloves garlic, crushed
2 carrots, sliced
2 sticks celery, sliced
2 bacon rashers, chopped
2 lb lean stewing beef stock
1 1/4 cups red wine
bouquet garni: parsley, bay, thyme
strip of orange peel
1 cup black olives
salt, pepper
flour (optional)

Preheat oven to 325°F. Heat olive oil in large flameproof casserole dish and brown first the vegetables and bacon, then the cubes of beef. Pour in the stock and wine, add the *bouquet garni* and orange peel. Cover, place in oven, and cook for about 3 hours, checking once or twice to see if liquid needs topping up. Add olives about 30 minutes before end of cooking time. Adjust seasoning with salt and pepper. If desired, the *daube* can be thickened with a thin paste of flour and water stirred in during the final 30 minutes of cooking.

Poulet Sauté aux Tomates

The seasonings of southern France – tomatoes, herbs and garlic – combined with chicken make a dish that contains the essence of Provence. If you can't get good sun-ripened tomatoes, canned tomatoes (drained) are preferable to flavorless hot-house ones.

---

1 roasting chicken, quartered
1 lemon, sliced in half
olive oil
1 shallot, chopped
1 clove garlic, finely chopped
1 lb tomatoes, peeled and chopped
2 tbsp chopped fresh herbs: tarragon, thyme, marjoram
2/3 cup chicken stock
2/3 cup white wine
salt, pepper

Rub the chicken with the cut lemon. Heat the olive oil in large pan and sauté the chicken until skin is golden. Turn skin side up, cover pan, and cook until chicken is done. Remove chicken and quickly sauté shallot and garlic in the pan. Return chicken to the pan and add remaining ingredients. Simmer uncovered until sauce is thickened. Season with salt and pepper and serve.

Sous Fassum

There are many versions of this recipe for stuffed cabbage and this one, from the Grasse-Antibes region, is said to have Roman origins. The tasty cooking liquid becomes soup to serve with the cabbage or as another meal.

1 large cabbage	1 lb sausages, cut up
2 tbsp olive oil	$\frac{1}{2}$ cup rice, uncooked
6 oz streaky bacon, chopped	$\frac{1}{3}$ cup raisins
2 onions, chopped	salt, pepper
2 cloves garlic, chopped	8-10 cups of
3 tomatoes, peeled and chopped	beef stock

(serves 6-8)

Bring a large pot of water to a boil. Remove damaged leaves from cabbage and cut out part of the core with a sharp knife. Put whole cabbage into boiling water until outer leaves are soft, about ten minutes. Plunge cabbage into cold water and drain. Line a bowl with a large piece of cheesecloth. Remove outer cabbage leaves and overlap them to line the bowl. Chop the cabbage heart and reserve.

For stuffing, heat olive oil and sauté the bacon, onions, and garlic. Add chopped cabbage heart, tomatoes, sausages, rice and raisins and remove from heat. Season with salt and pepper. Press stuffing into a ball and place in center of prepared cabbage leaves, pushing them together to enclose the stuffing completely. Pull up corners of the cloth and tie firmly. In a large pot, bring stock to boil, put in cabbage and simmer slowly for $2\frac{1}{2}$–3 hours.

Serve cut in wedges with a little of the soup poured over.

Zucchini Farcies

Savory stuffed vegetables glistening with olive oil are often served as a main course. Eggplant, tomatoes, peppers, and artichokes are all suitable candidates for this appetizing recipe.

---

4 medium zucchini
2–3 tbsp olive oil
1 onion, chopped
2 cloves garlic, chopped
2 mushrooms, chopped
2 tbsp finely chopped parsley
1–2 cups breadcrumbs
6 fillets of anchovy, chopped
pepper, salt

Preheat oven to 375°F. Split zucchini lengthwise, scoop out some of the flesh with a spoon and chop. Heat olive oil and sauté the onion, garlic, mushrooms, and chopped zucchini flesh until softened. Remove from heat and stir in remaining ingredients, using enough breadcrumbs to fill zucchini shells. Season well with black pepper and salt if needed. Fill zucchini with mixture, sprinkle with olive oil and place in a shallow dish with just enough water to cover bottom to depth of 1/4 inch. Bake in oven until zucchini are tender and stuffing is golden brown.

Ratatouille

Restaurant *ratatouille* can be a disappointing watery stew. In this Niçois version, vegetables are sautéed individually in olive oil and finally married with rich tomato sauce and herbs for a true Mediterranean taste.

---

1 lb tomatoes, peeled and chopped
3 cloves garlic, finely chopped
2 sprigs fresh thyme
pinch of sugar
2–3 tbsp olive oil
1 eggplant, peeled and diced
4 small zucchini, sliced
2 bell peppers, de-seeded and cut in strips
2 large onions, sliced
8–10 basil leaves, shredded
4 tbsp chopped parsley
salt, pepper

In a small pan over gentle heat, stew the tomatoes with the garlic, thyme, and sugar in a little olive oil. Meanwhile, in another pan heat more olive oil and sauté the eggplant, zucchini, bell peppers and onions in succession, removing each vegetable to a large pan as it is done. When tomatoes are reduced to thick sauce, combine with other vegetables and simmer together for 5 minutes. Season with salt and pepper and serve hot or cold.

Salade de Pois Chiches

Chick-peas are used in hot and cold dishes around the Mediterranean from Spain to the Middle East. Thrifty housewives use longer soaking time so that less cooking, and consequently less fuel, is required.

---

8 oz dried chick-peas
sprigs of thyme
juice of 1 lemon
2 cloves garlic, finely chopped
3 tbsp chopped parsley
6 tbsp olive oil
salt, pepper
1 onion, thinly sliced
handful of black olives

Soak chick-peas in water for 24–36 hours. Cook in fresh water with thyme, bringing quickly to a boil, then reducing heat to simmer 1½–2 hours, until tender. Meanwhile, combine lemon juice, garlic, parsley, olive oil, salt, and pepper in a jar and shake well to make dressing. Drain cooked chick-peas and pour dressing over while still hot. Stir in onion rings and black olives and allow to marinate before serving.

Tian d'Épinards

Spinach baked with rice and eggs serves as a vegetarian main course or accompaniment to plain grilled meat or fish. *Tians can be made of various vegetables and are named after the earthenware dish in which they are cooked.*

---

2 tbsp olive oil
I lb spinach leaves, chopped
I small onion, chopped
I clove garlic, chopped
I ¹/₂ cups cooked rice
3 eggs
³/₄ cup milk
salt, pepper
grated nutmeg

Preheat oven to 375°F. Heat olive oil in a pan with spinach, onion, and garlic. Stir until spinach is cooked in its own juices. Drain liquid if necessary, and combine with rice. Beat eggs and milk together, stir into spinach mixture and season with salt, pepper, and nutmeg. Pour into shallow, ovenproof dish and bake for about 25 minutes or until set.

Pain d'Olives

Good bread is an important part of the Provençal diet, often bought freshly baked twice a day. Flavored with olives and fresh herbs, it doesn't need butter, and makes a wonderful snack topped with *tapenade* (p. 24) or juicy slices of tomato and basil leaves. This easy recipe uses instant yeast which is blended with dry ingredients before liquid is added.

---

5 cups strong flour
1 tbsp fresh chopped herbs (optional)
2 tsp salt
4 tbsp olive oil
1 pkt instant yeast
2 cups warm water (approx.)
20 black olives, stoned and chopped
coarse sea salt

Preheat oven to 425°F. In a large bowl, mix together the flour, herbs, salt, olive oil, and yeast. Add enough warm water to make a soft dough and knead for a few minutes, until dough becomes elastic. Knead in the olives, form into an oval loaf, and place on a large oiled baking sheet. Cover with a plastic bag and leave in a warm place until doubled in size, 1 1/2 – 2 hours. Sprinkle loaf with sea salt and bake for about 25 minutes or until bread is golden brown and sounds hollow when tapped on bottom.

Pissaladière

A cousin of pizza, this version takes its name from *pissalat*, an old condiment of pounded fish macerated for a month with herbs and salt. Modern cooks use anchovies, and the bread dough can be made using half the recipe on page 47, omitting the black olives.

---

4 tbsp olive oil
2 lb onions, chopped
2 cloves garlic, chopped
1 tbsp chopped fresh herbs: oregano, thyme, rosemary
salt, pepper
1 lb bread dough (see p. 47)
1 can (2 oz) anchovy fillets, drained
24 black olives

Preheat oven to 375°F. Heat olive oil in a heavy-bottomed pan and sweat the onions and garlic over very gentle heat with the lid on for about an hour, stirring occasionally. The onions should reduce to a purée without browning. Stir in herbs during final 15 minutes of cooking and add salt and pepper. Oil a 12–inch pizza pan with hands, then stretch and press the dough to line pan, pinching up a raised edge. Spread onions over the dough, lay anchovies over the onions in a lattice pattern, and place an olive in the center of each diamond. Leave covered to rise for about 30 minutes, then bake for about 25 minutes, until dough is cooked through and golden. Serve hot.

Pan Bagna

This "bathed bread" is literally dripping with olive oil, garlic, and the other good things that are the essence of Provençal flavors. These fragrant morsels are delicious accompaniments to drinks.

I can (2 oz) anchovy fillets
2 cloves garlic, crushed
4 tbsp olive oil
I tbsp lemon juice
I long French bread loaf
I onion, thinly sliced
shredded red and green bell peppers
I sliced boiled egg
tomato slices
fresh basil leaves (optional)
black pepper

In a small saucepan, heat together the anchovy fillets and their oil with the garlic, olive oil, and lemon juice, mashing with a spoon until anchovies are melted into the sauce. Split the bread lengthwise and brush each side with a little of the warm sauce. Layer the onions, peppers, sliced egg and tomatoes on one bread half, drizzle over the remaining sauce, and cover with the top half. Wrap in foil or plastic wrap, weight with a heavy chopping board or plate and leave for at least an hour for bread to soak up the juices. Cut in 1-inch slices to serve.

Tomates Provençales en Salade

The fresh taste of sun-ripened tomatoes is enhanced by the simplest of Provençal seasonings in this salad, which improves when made ahead to allow flavors to mingle. Serve with bread to soak up the delicious juices.

---

large bunch of parsley
2 cloves garlic
6 large ripe tomatoes
salt, pepper
red wine vinegar
olive oil

Chop the parsley and garlic together very finely. Cut tomatoes into thick slices and layer into dish with chopped parsley, sprinkling each layer with salt, pepper, a little vinegar, and olive oil. Cover and leave to marinate in a cool place for at least an hour before serving.

Tourte de Blettes

Tender leaves of swiss chard provide the base for this unusual sweet tart made with raisins, cheese, and nuts. If the tart is to be served as an *hors d'oeuvre*, use less sugar.

---

shortcrust pastry for double-crust tart
$^1/_2$ cup raisins
2 tbsp marc or rum
4 large dessert apples, peeled, cored and sliced
3 cups cooked and chopped swiss chard
5 tbsp brown sugar
$^1/_2$ cup pine kernels
$^3/_4$ cup grated cheddar
grated rind of 1 lemon
2 eggs, beaten
cream (optional)

Preheat oven to 375°F. Heat raisins in the marc or rum and leave to soak while filling is prepared. In a large bowl, combine all the remaining ingredients, except pastry, mix well and add raisins and their soaking liquid. Roll pastry to specified size and thickness and line 10-inch tart pan. Put in filling. Roll pastry top. Cover filling with pastry top, moisten edges, and press together edges of pastry base to seal. Slash the top in several places, place on baking sheet, and bake 45–50 minutes. Serve hot or warm with cream.

Tarte au Potiron

The golden pumpkins of late summer are used in the south as vegetables or dessert. This tart made with almonds and pumpkin forms part of the traditional *treize desserts*, the thirteen sweets of Christmas.

$^{7}/_{8}$ cup blanched almonds, toasted
$^{1}/_{2}$ cup sugar
strip of orange peel
$1^{1}/_{4}$ cups pumpkin purée
$^{1}/_{2}$ tsp mixed ground spice: cinnamon, nutmeg, cloves
1 beaten egg
12 oz puff pastry

Preheat oven to 350°F. In a blender, grind together the almonds, sugar, and orange peel. Remove to a bowl and combine with pumpkin and mixed spice. Reserve 1 tablespoonful of the beaten egg and stir the remainder into pumpkin mixture. Roll out pastry to line 8–inch tart pan and spoon in filling. Cut remaining pastry into strips, moisten with reserved beaten egg, and arrange in lattice over top. Brush tart with reserved beaten egg and bake until pastry is golden and filling is set, about 25-30 minutes.

Ratafia d'Oranges

Provence is famous for its candied fruit and citrus peels. The fragrant peel of southern oranges is also excellent flavoring for *ratafia*, the term applied to liqueurs made from cognac rather than white alcohol. It should be made at least one month in advance.

---

6 large oranges
2 cups sugar
4 1/4 cups cognac
1 inch piece of cinnamon bark
8 coriander seeds, slightly bruised

Peel the orange zest very thinly so there is no trace of white pith and cut into narrow strips. Squeeze juice from peeled oranges, strain and combine with other ingredients in a jar. Cover tightly, shake to help dissolve the sugar, and leave in a dark, cool place to infuse for at least a month, turning from time to time. To use, strain off into a clean bottle or decanter.

Index